WHAT EVERYONE SHOULD KNOW
ABOUT JUDAISM

What Everyone Should Know About Judaism

Answers to the Questions
Most Frequently Asked
About Judaism

By

Rabbi Morton M. Applebaum

Foreword by

JOHN HAYNES HOLMES

PHILOSOPHICAL LIBRARY

New York

to
ELEANOR and our children
LOIS JEAN, AND BRUCE JAY

FOREWORD

I am happy in having the opportunity herewith, thanks to the hospitality of my friend and colleague, the author of this book, to state my judgment as to its worth. I think that its worth is very high, and I am glad, therefore, that it is to be published in permanent form.

This volume was originally intended, I understand, to be an essay on Basic Judaism. But Judaism exists not alone in the world. It's all inwrought in the tragic history both of our eastern and western worlds through lingering centuries of time. Any attempt to explain the content of Jewish thought and life must inevitably overflow, so to speak, into Christianity which is so deeply rooted in Jewish sources. Christianity and Judaism, not to speak of other great religions of the world, are so definitely a part of one another as to be inseparable. They cannot be torn apart, representing as they do a single dispensation of the spirit.

Rabbi Applebaum has done wisely in extending the area of his discussion. In this regard he is following in the footsteps of Isaiah who found it necessary, or at least advisable, to exhort his people Israel to "enlarge the place of thy tent, and stretch forth the curtains of thy habitation . . . to lengthen thy cords and strengthen thy stakes."

What I am trying to say is that "basic Judaism" is basic Christianity as well. The book, Rabbi Applebaum's little masterpiece, has a dual value which belongs to the Jewish and Christian tradition together. How easily and appropriately the Old Testament (a Jewish document) fits into the New Testament (a Christian document) which are the component parts of that great unity, the Bible! What the Rabbi

vii

has written with such sympathy and understanding belongs to us both, we can share and share alike.

Of the character and worth of this book it's unnecessary to speak in this place. It must be left to each solitary reader to discover what belongs to him, on the one hand, and to the Judeo-Christian tradition, on the other. It's a noble heritage as deep as time and as sacred as the word of God.

John Haynes Holmes

Minister Emeritus
The Community Church
of New York

PREFACE

This book is for JEWS and NON-JEWS. It deals with answers to the questions most frequently asked by non-Jews about Judaism—the same answers which Jews ought to know not only to avoid the embarrassment of inability to answer the questions of their non-Jewish friends, but as a matter of their own education as Jews.

The questions were asked of the writer over a period of years on Jewish Chautauqua Society engagements at colleges and church camps which frequently requested his lecture on "WHAT EVERY CHRISTIAN OUGHT TO KNOW ABOUT JUDAISM." Christian clergy, church groups, Public School teachers, PTAs, Hi Y Teens, Service clubs like Rotary, Kiwanis and Lions, also favored this topic. The presentation was usually followed by a question and answer period. The questions manifested a profound interest in, and considerable familiarity with, things Jewish. Reactions to the answers were interesting.

From one Rotarian, a Christian gentleman, came the comment, "If only I had had the opportunity to learn such facts about twenty years ago, how much better would I have understood my Jewish friends and business associates."

Jewish groups were interested in "WHAT CHRISTIANS WANT TO KNOW ABOUT JUDAISM," and asked their questions.

Mr. Craig Wilson, religious editor of the Akron Beacon Journal, submitted ten questions for answers which were featured in his column.

From all of these, the writer formulated a list of "One Hundred Questions on Basic Judaism." It was called to the attention of the Union of American Hebrew Congregations by Rabbi Jerome D. Folkman of Columbus, Ohio, and was subsequently published in the December 1954 issue of AMERICAN JUDAISM, its official publication. The list was reprinted in many Anglo-Jewish periodicals both in the United States and Canada, and many of their readers began writing in for the answers.

In the summer of 1958, the writer was urged by Mr. Sylvan Lebow, Executive Director of the National Federation of Temple Brotherhoods, to prepare the answers for inclusion in an Adult Education Kit which his organization was preparing for distribution.

Mindful of the limited time which the average reader has for reading, and recalling the preference of one of my College History professors for examination answers that were "brief but in detail," and satisfied that there *are* virtues in brevity and precision, I sought to so answer the One Hundred Questions. To be sure, encapsulated facts are no substitute for wisdom which requires intensive reading and research. Yet, with so much to read, there are the many who do welcome a combination of conciseness and accuracy in the presentation of information. In truth, as one has observed, "Brief statements very often take much longer than the preparation of a full essay." In any event, I made simplicity and succinctness my objective in this work, and deliberately avoided overburdening it with notes and quotes.

The National Federation of Temple Brotherhoods, shortly after the distribution of the kit to its clubs reported having received "many favorable reactions and indications that it (the material in this book) is being put to good use," and that there were many recommendations and requests that it be made available in book form. Further encouragement came from colleagues and laymen—Jews and

Christians—who had read the material and considered it, "meaty . . . admirably done . . . very deserving of printing and wide distribution . . . Christians and Jews will welcome it . . . very helpful as a Confirmation Class refresher course in basic Judaism . . . a valuable aid to prospective converts."

In preparing the material for publication, the author added a few more questions to his original list; subheaded a few, as they are usually phrased by Christians; and enlarged upon many of the answers. Instead of offering his own answers to the questions dealing with the various branches of Judaism, he solicited and selected such from scholarly and representative interpreters. Indebtedness is therefore acknowledged to RANDOM HOUSE, New York, for permission to quote from THE WISDOM OF ISRAEL by Lewis Browne, from the chapter on "Practices of Orthodox Judaism," to BEHRMAN HOUSE, INC. PUBLISHERS, New York, for permission to quote from REFORM JUDAISM—A Guide for Reform Jews, by Rabbi Abraham J. Feldman; to THE BURNING BUSH PRESS, New York, for permission to quote from TRADITION AND CHANGE—The Development of Conservative Judaism, by Rabbi Mordecai Waxman; and to Dr. Mordecai M. Kaplan for his statement on Reconstructionism. THE HEBREW UNION COLLEGE PRESS, Cincinnati, has likewise been kind in granting permission to quote from A JEWISH UNDERSTANDING OF THE NEW TESTAMENT by Dr. Samuel Sandmel.

The writer would also here record his profound thanks to Mr. Sylvan Lebow and the National Federation of Temple Brotherhoods for their interest and encouragement in the publication of this work. He has also benefitted from the reading, suggestions and encouragement of several of his colleagues, in particular Rabbi Samuel M. Silver, Editor of AMERICAN JUDAISM, New York; Dr. Sylvan D. Schwartzman, Professor of Education at the Hebrew Union College—Jewish Institute of Religion, Cincinnati, Ohio; and Dr. John Haynes Holmes, Minister Emeritus of the Community Church of New York, who has also written the Foreword. His thanks include those to his secretaries, Miss Lois Salpeter and Mrs. Murray Cohen, for their kindness and diligence in preparing the typescript.

I trust that this "book of brevity" will be found helpful and valuable as a compendium of WHAT EVERYONE SHOULD KNOW ABOUT JUDAISM.

Morton M. Applebaum

Temple Israel
Akron, Ohio

CONTENTS

II. JEWISH SOURCES

III. HOLY DAYS AND HOLIDAYS

IV. IN TEMPLE AND SYNAGOGUE

(See also answers to questions on pages 22 and 23.)

V. LIFE CYCLE CEREMONIES

VI. GENERAL

EPILOGUE

WHAT EVERYONE SHOULD KNOW
ABOUT JUDAISM

I. NON-JEWS INVARIABLY ASK

How Would You Define Judaism?

Judaism is the religion of the Jewish people *plus* the set of insights acquired by Jews as the result of their religious teachings, their cultural explorations and their vicissitudes over the course of years.

Actually there is no single definition acceptable to all Jews. Different points of view account for a variety of definitions. Some maintain that Judaism is solely a religion. Some define it as a civilization; others as a nationality; still others as a religio-culture.

How Would You Define Hebrew?

The word Hebrew (*Ivri* in Hebrew) is an ancient name used to designate the Jews. Some scholars associate the word with the Hebrew word *avar*—to cross, and link it to Abraham who in coming to Canaan from Haran crossed the river Euphrates. Abraham became known as the man from beyond the river—*b'ever ha-nahar*. Since the Jewish people began with Abraham, they were called Hebrews.

Dr. Julian L. Levy, a celebrated Semiticist, is of the opinion that Hebrew originally meant "a newcomer."

How Would You Define Israelite?

Originally, Israel was the name applied to Jacob after the episode in which the patriarch wrestled with the invisible force (Genesis 32.28). Etymologically, the word Israel means Champion of God. Homiletically, this seems to refer to the fact that Jacob wrestled with his lower impulses and overcame them. Because the Jews are the descendants of Jacob, they are often called the sons of Jacob or Israelites. As most people know, the Jewish republic in Palestine is called Israel. Jews who live in the State of Israel are called "Israeli Jews." Jews who live elsewhere are nationally designated according to the country in which they reside and of which they are citizens either by birth or naturalization.

How Would You Define Jew?

The word "Jew," is derived from "Judah," the southern part of Palestine. After most of the ten tribes of Northern Israel disappeared, Jews came principally from Judah. The word "Judah" after having undergone a succession of Aramaic, Greek, Latin, French and English changes resulted in the word "Jew," applied to those who were of the people who came from Judah. The term refers primarily to one who adheres to the Jewish faith but also includes non-religious Jews who have been born into the Jewish group.

What Is a "Cohen"?

A "Cohen" is a presumed descendant of the priestly family of Aaron.

While many Jews bear the name "Cohen" or any of the

4

linguistic variations thereof ("Cohn," "Cohane," "Kahn," "Kagan," etc.) as a surname, the name is more a designation of the hereditary priestly office than a surname. Whether all who bear the name "Cohen" are directly descended from Aaron is subject to question.

Are the Jews a Race?

No! Jews are found among all races. There is no distinct and separate Jewish "race" in any scientific sense of the term. This is the consensus of leading anthropologists and ethnologists. Racially speaking, Jews are considered to be "essentially a mixture of the Syrian-Anatolian branch of the Alpine race and the Eastern branch of the Mediterranean race."

The "mixture" which is the Jewish People today is best seen in the State of Israel, whither have come Jews from all parts of the globe: "ivory Jews from Eastern and Central Europe; blue-eyed blonds from Scandinavia; yellow-skinned from China; black-skinned from the Sudan; light brown from Yemen; deeply tanned from Morocco; milk-chocolate from India;" tall and short; long-headed and short-headed; straight hair and curly; pug nosed and hooked—just every kind.

How Does One Become a Jew?

One who is born to Jewish parents is a Jew by birth. Those who are not Jews by birth may become Jews by choice, by being converted to Judaism. Traditionalist rabbis require that male proselytes be circumcised, and that females go through the initiatory rite of the *mikvah*, ritual bath.

Reform rabbis may accept into the sacred covenant of Israel any honorable and intelligent person who desires such affiliation of his or her free-will and choice to embrace Judaism. A course of study is followed by a Service of Conversion. A certificate of conversion, properly signed by the rabbi and countersigned by two witnesses, is given to the convert.

Why Don't Jews Solicit Converts?

Part of the answer has been given by one of the ablest Christian scholars on Judaism, Professor George Foote Moore, in his classic work *Judaism*. There (Vol. I, page 352) he points out that "Christian emperors, when Christianity became the State Religion made conversions to Judaism a crime in itself with increasingly severe penalties both for the Christian convert and the Jew who converted him." Thus did the rise of Christianity mark the decline of active proselytism on the part of the Jewish people.

When Moses Mendelssohn, in the latter part of the 18th century, was asked this same question, he replied, "The duty to proselytize springs clearly from the idea that outside of a certain belief there is no salvation. I, as a Jew, am not bound to accept that dogma, because according to the teachings of our rabbis, 'The righteous of all people shall have part in the rewards of the future world.'" This is to say that based upon rabbinical teachings, Judaism claims no monopoly on salvation. Judaism reasons that whatever "the rewards of the future world" may be, all God-revering people will share therein. The righteous Christian and Mohammedan will share equally with the righteous Jew in those rewards whatever they may be. Judaism does not claim for its beliefs the truth, the whole truth, and nothing but the truth. Furthermore, Jews are taught to respect any religion which is sound in its moral teaching even though they differ with its theology. In this feeling, Judaism could, as it did, withdraw from the field of proselytizing.

Although Jews do not seek converts, they do welcome them.

Do Jews Still Regard Themselves as the "Chosen People"?

Widely misunderstood, this phrase merely signifies two facts:

    a. Judaism was the first to give the world an inkling of the significance of monotheism, and

    b. Judaism feels it has an assignment, a *raison d'etre*, a religious mission.

According to the concept articulated by Isaiah, the Jews *are* chosen not to domineer, but to serve; not to rule, but to teach; not to proselytize, but to ethicize.

What Is the "Mission Idea" in Judaism?

The "Mission Idea" originated with the Hebrew prophets who developed the thesis that Jews have a divine errand: to bring the nations of the world to understand that God wants men to use their faculties for the hastening of an era bright with brotherhood and peace. See Isaiah Chapter 42, notably verse 6 and following: "I the Lord have called thee in righteousness, And have taken hold of thy hand, And kept thee, and set thee for a covenant of the people, For a light of the nations; To open the blind eyes," etc.

————

What Is the Jewish Attitude Towards Mixed Marriage and Intermarriage?

Judaism makes a distinction between "intermarriage" and "mixed marriage." By "intermarriage" we understand a marriage contracted between two people, originally of different faiths, where one converts to the faith of the other. By "mixed marriage" we understand a marriage of two people of different religious backgrounds who, in marriage, retain separate religious affiliations.

While Judaism definitely encourages its followers to find their mates in their own religious household, intermarriages are performed and blessed. This is to say that free-will converts are accepted into Judaism and after conversion will be married to another Jew by a rabbi. The feeling is that mixed marriages are hazardous and not sound and they are, therefore, discouraged.

Would You Say That Judaism, Like Christianity, Owes Its Existence to Any One Individual?

No! Judaism owes its existence to the Jewish people, to countless individuals and influences. Judaism has been shaped by patriarchs and judges, priests and prophets, psalmists and scribes, rabbis and sages, poets and philosophers, mystics and moralists, preachers and teachers, and also by the civilizations with which it came into contact and from which it borrowed. Not even Moses is indispensable to Judaism. Judaism depends upon insights which it believes are being constantly revealed to men.

When Was Judaism Revealed?

"Revealed" is hardly the right term. Judaism is traditionally believed to have begun with the discovery by Abraham (about 1500 B.C.E.) that the world is a unit, governed by a Divine Force which seeks to prod man upwards to higher moral behavior, ergo, the worship of the One God. To the first patriarch's religious discoveries were added others of those who came after him, making Judaism a continuous development spanning the centuries from Abraham to our own time.

Do All Jews Believe Alike?

No. There are three interpretations: Reform, Conservatism and Orthodoxy. Actually there are *two* strains: the Traditionalist and the Liberal. Orthodoxy tends to glorify the past and resist changes. Reform believes that authentic Judaism is one which modifies its practices in accordance with new needs. Conservatism is in between. Existing differences, in the main, derive from the authority ascribed to Jewish tradition and the degree to which Liberal and Traditionalist incline to, or decline from, reinterpreting beliefs and adjusting practices to modern thinking and living. (See further.)

––––––––

What Is Orthodox Judaism?

"One of the basic difficulties you will experience in getting orthodox Rabbis to define orthodox Judaism," wrote one of its leading interpreters in answer to the writer's request for such a statement, "is that they start with the premise that orthodox Judaism is Judaism . . ."

A "brief but in detail" answer to this question has it as follows: "It is fundamentally ritualistic, insisting that the practices ordained in the Pentateuch, and amplified in the Talmud and the later rabbinic Codes, are still sacrosanct and binding. It recognizes a distinction between *dinim* ("laws") which are mandatory, and *minhagim* ("customs") which are volitional; but it tends to lay equal emphasis on both. This is because the basic aim is to keep the Jew from yielding to the gravitational forces exerted by his Gen-

10

tile environment, and such an aim can best be served by making his personal conduct ubiquitously distinctive. Orthodox Judaism is thus more than a creed; it is a way of life."

—Lewis Browne
(in THE WISDOM OF ISRAEL, page 707)

————

What Is Reform Judaism?

The following was written by Dr. Abraham J. Feldman, Rabbi of Congregation Beth Israel of Hartford, Connecticut, a Past-President of the Central Conference of American Rabbis, the national association of Reform Rabbis.

"Reform Judaism is a Jewish religious movement originating in Germany in the 18th century. It has sought and continues to seek so to interpret Judaism that it may meet the religious needs of the Jew in modern times. It clings to the basic concepts of historical Judaism. But it has made changes in some customs and ceremonies which have come to us from the past. In doing this, Reform Judaism remained true to the spirit and practice of traditional historic Judaism which, be it remembered, has always been both adaptable and progressive.

"When we speak of Reform Judaism we are not speaking of a new kind of Judaism. It was only the name that was new as it came into being near the end of the 18th century in Germany. This name has become the label of that interpretation of Judaism which recognizes and emphasizes the dynamic character of the Jewish religion—*dynamic,* which is the opposite of arrested or static Judaism. Reform Judaism

11

emphasizes what is inherent in all Judaism, the principle of progression in the concepts and forms of the Jewish religion. Reform has its roots in the past! It proudly acknowledges the glory, the dignity, the validity of Jewish tradition. It chooses to continue to identify itself with the tradition and it refuses to admit that Jewish tradition is something which is petrified, the crystallization of any one moment or era of Jewish religious thought and experience. This idea of a progressive Jewish tradition is not new. The Jewish tradition always was progressive but, especially in the 15th through the 18th centuries, an effort was made to freeze it. When the ghetto disappeared and the period of emancipation began, this frozen tradition failed to hold and to satisfy those generations because of its completely unbending and, in a very real sense, unorthodox position. It was then that a group of Jews, led by laymen at first, decided that it was time to unfreeze the tradition, and attempted the long overdue and the long dammed-up adjustments. This was the beginning of the modern Reform. The Reformers did not seek escape from Judaism. If they had, the road was open and a welcome awaited them elsewhere. They *wanted* to remain within the fold and orbit of Judaism but they wanted the tradition unfrozen and the processes of change speeded up."

—From REFORM JUDAISM,
A Guide for Reform Jews
by Rabbi Abraham J. Feldman

12

What Is Conservative Judaism?

Conservative Judaism, as a movement in America, may be said to have begun with the founding of the Jewish Theological Seminary of America in New York in 1887, followed by the organization of the United Synagogue in 1913 "to join together the congregations affiliated with the Seminary."

The ideology of Conservative Judaism has been described by Rabbi Mordecai Waxman, one of its young leaders, as follows:

"The ideology of Conservative Judaism is more a matter of emphasis than of a radically new doctrine . . .

1. The founders of Conservative Judaism had no intention of starting a new wing or denomination or party in Judaism. They did not even pretend to be modern Judaism. Their purpose and philosophy were clearly expressed in the name they applied to themselves. They were conservative and their object was to conserve the Jewish traditions . . . were all scrupulous in asserting that they represented a tendency and not a party. They conceived of their role as that of presenting an organized and meaningful alternative to the Reform movement . . .

The Conservative movement has always clung to the position that it is not a denomination in the Jewish fold. It holds that it *is* Judaism. It is the Jewish tradition continuing along its path in time and space with characteristic dynamism. . . While it recognizes that Orthodoxy and Reform play a significant role in Jewish life, it feels that Reform is a revolutionary deviation from Jewish tradition and that

13

Orthodoxy, in stultifying the inner dynamism of Judaism, has taken itself on to a side path of Jewish life. To itself it assigns the role of being the staunch upholder of the Jewish tradition and of its inherent dynamism.

2. In making the conservation of the Jewish tradition their objective, the founders and leaders of Conservative Judaism were not blind to the pressures created by the American Jewish scene and by the modern world. They recognized that the survival of Judaism was imperilled by non-observance, by ignorance, and by intellectual confusion. But they were not prepared to make these factors the determinants of what Judaism is and should be. The Conservative movement has not really been a mass phenomenon even though it has attracted the loyalty of a great number of Jews. It has sought to shape the community rather than allow the community to shape it. Its thinking and goals have been derived from the Jewish tradition rather than from the doctrinaire or sociological forces. It feels that the Jewish community is malleable, that it is reclaimable and that it is, potentially at least, devoted to Judaism. The problem, as it sees it, is to state Judaism in meaningful terms, to focus attention on its essentials and to communicate these things to the Jewish public.

Starting from these underlying principles, that the Jewish tradition must be preserved and conserved, and that American Jewry must be moulded to that end, Conservative Judaism evolved not a doctrine, but a technique."

—Rabbi Mordecai Waxman (in TRADITION AND CHANGE: The Development of Conservative Judaism, page 12 ff)

What Is Reconstructionism?

An outlook on Jewish life and a movement begun by Dr. Mordecai M. Kaplan, celebrated professor of the Jewish Theological Seminary. According to Kaplan, Judaism is a civilization, with many religious and cultural values and institutions, all of which ought to be centrally promoted, democratically governed and underwritten by all those who want to be known as Jews. Kaplan argues against the "anarchy" which prevails in Jewish life, and asks for a "reconstruction" of the American Jewish community, as the predominant force in Jewish life.

* * * * *

The following was penned on July 21, 1958, by Dr. Morde-cai M. Kaplan at the request of the writer, in answer to the question, "What is Reconstructionism?"

". . . Reconstructionism tries to be more in keeping with the realities and needs of human life than any of the existing versions of Judaism. It takes exception to Orthodoxy's supernaturalism, to Conservative's legalistic approach to ritual practice, and to Reform's misconception of Judaism as a religion analagous to Christianity, and of the Jews as a religious community like the Church.

"Actually Judaism is more inclusive than the Jewish religion. It is nothing less than the evolving religious civilization of the Jewish People. To live as a Jew, therefore, means to be aware of belonging to the Jewish People, with all the responsibilities that go with such belonging. It means to share the history, the destiny and the contemporary vicissi-

15

tudes of the Jewish People, in the spirit of its evolving religion.

"In the light of what we now know concerning the normal relationship of a people to its religion, Jewish religion is likely to degenerate into a way of speaking from the pulpit, that is without any influence on the daily conduct of its adherents. The only way to counteract that tendency is to afford the Jewish religion an opportunity of becoming an integral part of a full-fledged Jewish civilization. That is possible only in Israel.

"Despite the contention, however, of some Zionists, Reconstructionism affirms that also outside Israel it is possible for Jews to maintain at least a cadre—the essential frame—of Jewish civilization, together with its Jewish religion. Even in that reduced form, Judaism can well provide its adherents all the ethical, esthetic and spiritual values necessary to elicit from them their highest potentialities as human beings. . . ."

———

Who Were the Pharisees?

Called in Hebrew *P'rushim,* from the word meaning "to separate" or "to examine," the Pharisees were sages who kept Judaism alive while Rome ruled Palestine and helped it survive after the Dispersion. They were "separatists" in the sense that they sought to keep the Jewish people separate from paganism. As "examiners," they examined the Biblical laws to determine which might be interpreted to remain applicable for their times and changing conditions. The Pharisees contributed much to the Talmud. Much of the misunderstanding about them in non-Jewish circles stems from their portrayal in the New Testament. Christian scholars, themselves, are today beginning to recognize the unjustified treatment of them by the Gospel writers inasmuch as many of the teachings of Jesus were Pharisaic.

――――――

What Do Jews Believe About Jesus?

Judaism is strictly a monotheistic faith rooted in the commandment, "I am the Lord thy God . . . thou shalt have no other gods before Me." Jewish commitment to this concept of unshared unity is uncompromising. The Jewish Confession of Faith makes clear, "Hear, O Israel: the Lord our God, the Lord is One."

The distinction is made between the "Jewish Jesus" and the "Christian Christ." Jews can respect Jesus whose Hebrew name was Joshua or Jeshua, for the Jew that he was, a preacher and teacher of Jewish ethics. Jews can accept him as a "good man" but not as a "God-man." Jews believe that all human beings are divine, for the "spirit born of God's spirit is breathed into all His children to animate and to ennoble all of them." According to this reasoning, Jesus was divine, but no more nor less than any of God's children. The apotheosis of Jesus is inconsonant with the Jewish belief in absolute monotheism.

Do Jews Still Look Forward to the Coming of the Messiah?

The answer includes a "yes" and a "no." Traditionalists entertain a belief in some kind of a personal deliverer to be sent to earth by God. Liberal Jews have given up the belief in a personal Messiah, but subscribe to the conviction that man has it within him to create a messianic period on earth. Most modern Jews think in terms of such a messianic age of brotherhood and peace to be realized by cooperative and combined human effort rather than by that of any single individual.

——————

Did Isaiah Predict the Coming of a Messiah?

No. What is often cited as such a prediction is merely a statement that events would take a decided turn in a period during which a woman could conceive and give birth to a child, and rear it to the point when it could tell good from evil (See Isaiah 7.16). Isaiah did project a messianic hope of moral and religious regeneration. He looked forward to one of the house of David, an ideal king to supplant the unworthy rulers and usher in the reign of everlasting peace and justice. He did not predict the coming of a theological Messiah.

Is There Any Basis Upon Which Jews May Celebrate Christmas?

No. Certainly its religious elements cannot properly command the allegiance or acceptance of a Jew who believes in monotheism and rejects the divinity of Jesus. Naturally, the general spirit of good fellowship which prevails during the long Christmas season can be enjoyed and admired by Jews.

Why Do Jews Rush the Burial of Their Dead?

Not all Jews do. Orthodox Jews are accustomed to burying their dead within 24 hours where possible, except on the Sabbath and certain holidays. The custom grows out of the practice not to embalm the dead. To embalm is to retard the process of disintegration. Orthodox Judaism believes that with complete disintegration, the return of dust unto dust and full atonement attained, the soul is free to be on its way. In the absence of embalming and because of rapid disintegration, Orthodox Jews hasten the burial of their dead.

Non-Orthodox Jews have no objection to embalming and therefore do not rush the burial of their dead. Such find support for their practice in the Biblical references to the embalming of Jacob and of Joseph (Genesis 50.2-3;26).

Do Jews Permit Cremation?

Liberal Jews do; traditionalist Jews do not. The latter retain an historic antagonism towards this practice, regarding it as a violation of a positive precept "to bury the dead," and running counter to the belief in the resurrection of the body. The position and practice of Reform Judaism is in accordance with the resolution of the Central Conference of American Rabbis (1892) "that in case we should be invited to officiate as ministers of religion at the cremation of a departed coreligionist, we ought not to refuse on the plea that cremation is anti-Jewish or irreligious."

What Do Jews Believe About Salvation and Life After Death?

The doctrines of salvation and life after death do not preoccupy Jewish thinking as much as they do Christian thinking. Judaism's concern is more with life in the "here" than in the "hereafter," with "this worldly" opportunities rather than with speculation about "the furniture of heaven and the temperature of hell."

However, the traditional Jew does believe in some kind of physical resurrection preceding a great Day of Judgment. The modern Jewish belief is in spiritual immortality, that is, that the soul is immortal. The reasoning behind the latter is that the soul, as the animating spark of human life, being divine, is *ipso facto* eternal and immortal. This belief rests upon the further reasoning that the soul when separated from the body, returns unto God, the Fountainhead of all spirits.

What Is the Jewish Conception of Sin?

Judaism regards sin as the opposite of good. It believes that each individual has innate moral freedom to choose between good and evil, that within each there are two inclinations— the good and the bad. The charge and challenge are that we "subdue the evil and strive after ideal ends." Failure to subdue the evil results in sin. Judaism has nothing like the Christian belief in Original Sin.

What Is a Rabbi?

"Rabbi" is the Hebrew for "my teacher." Rabbis are not priests. They do not serve as intermediaries between God and the people unto whom they minister. They are professional laymen academically trained to teach and interpret Judaism. This is their first and foremost function. But the role of the rabbi includes preaching, pastoral ministration, congregational administration, communal leadership, et cetera. Rabbis are today both university and seminary trained, possessing both secular and religious knowledge. They are ordained by seminaries with the degree of "Rabbi," and are on their own thereafter. There is no rabbinical hierarchy which has charge of rabbinical placement and to whom individual rabbis are responsible. There are national rabbinical associations to which one may or may not choose to belong. Yes, rabbis may, and do, marry, and have families.

What Is It That Jews Fasten on Their Doors?

The small receptacle attached to the door is called a *mezuzah,* the Hebrew word meaning "doorpost." Inside the wooden or metal tube is a rolled rectangular piece of parchment containing the Biblical passages about the mezuzah (Deuteronomy 6.4-9 and 11.13-21), including the *Shema Yisroel* ("Hear, O Israel . . .") and the *V'ahavtah* ("And thou shalt love . . ."). The word *Shaddai,* "Almighty One," is visible on the face of the mezuzah.

It was created in the distant past as a fit symbol and aid to fulfill the divine injunction: "And thou shalt write them upon the doorposts of thy house, and upon thy gates." (Deuteronomy 6.9) The mezuzah is affixed in a slanting position to the upper part of the right-hand doorpost. The pious are accustomed, as they pass it, to lay a kiss with the hand upon it as they utter the prayer: "May God watch over my going out and my coming in from this time forth and for evermore."

Because *mezuzos* (plural) came to be thought of as good-luck amulets, Reform Judaism relinquished them. However, more and more of them are being used nowadays, even by Liberal Jews, as a fitting Jewish home identification and as a symbol of God's presence in family life.

————

Why Do Some Jews Worship with Heads Covered and Others with Heads Uncovered?

Neither the Bible nor the Talmud specifies whether Jews should pray with headcovering. Gradually, Jewish people adopted and adapted themselves to the prevailing Eastern practice of donning headcovering as a mark of respect, and worship was conducted in that way. Most liberal Jews have dispensed with headcovering at prayer on the grounds that in Western countries respect is shown by removing the hat. Actually, the wearing of headcovering is optional in liberal synagogues.

What Is a "Yarmulka"?

It is the Slavic term for a "skullcap."

Why Is There an Organ in a Temple but Not in an Orthodox Synagogue?

Originally, as we can see in the Book of Psalms, musical instruments accompanied the worship in the ancient Temple. After it was destroyed in 70 C.E., it was decreed that music should no longer be played in the synagogues. This was decreed as a sign of mourning for the great sanctuary and in accordance with the view that the entire priestly apparatus would be restored miraculously with the advent of the Messiah. Reform Judaism broke with the view that a personal Messiah was coming and with the corollary that aspects of the worship in the ancient Temple must be suspended. Therefore, they re-instituted instrumental music in the house of worship, which they deliberately designated Temple, to indicate that they regard it as the successor of the ancient shrine.

23

Why Do Some Jews Change Their Names?

In some cases to shorten or simplify Old World names (many "Jewish" names are German or Slavic); in other cases to escape identity as Jews. It is also interesting to note that in Israel Jews are "Hebraizing" their names (Green to Ben Gurion, Chertok to Sharett, etc.).

There also is an ancient Jewish custom to add to the name of a sick person a suitable one picked from the Bible. The added name becomes the sick person's first name. According to the superstitious, adding a name causes an evil decree to be cancelled.

Do All Jews Look Forward to Returning to Israel?

No. But Jews *now* do have the choice. Israel's doors are open to them. But the vast majority of Jews who enjoy physical and psychological security in lands where their roots are firmly fixed manifest no desire or intention to migrate to Israel.

What Is the Jewish Idea of God?

He is One, the Creator, the Unknowable source of life, the Father of all, eternal, incorporeal, omnipotent, omnipresent, omniscient, the Divine Urger of higher morality, the Implanter of good potentialities, the Granter of free will by which man may choose to activate his good qualities

24

instead of succumbing to his bad ones, and also He Who reveals Himself in the experience of the Jewish People.

What Does "Kosher" Mean?

The Hebrew word *Kosher* means "ritually proper." It designates, for those who observe the Jewish dietary laws, that which is permissible for eating. See Leviticus, Chapter 11 and Deuteronomy, Chapter 14. From the general dietary commands of the Bible there evolved the Talmudic detailed regulations concerning permissible and forbidden foods, and ritual slaughter.

The permissible foods include: all plant products, quadrupeds possessing cloven hoofs and chewing their cud, flesh of birds (except birds of prey), fish with scales and fins, milk and eggs (except of forbidden animals, birds and fish), and honey. For meat to be "kosher," the animal or fowl must be ritually slaughtered and prepared.

The forbidden foods are designated as "traif," the Hebrew word actually meaning "to tear to pieces;" its Mishnaic and Talmudic sense "to be declared unfit for food." Such include pig (specifically prohibited by the Bible), shellfish, blood, and the mixture of meat and milk products. The latter is based upon the thrice repeated prohibition found in Exodus 23.19, 34.26, and Deuteronomy 14.21, against "seething a kid in its mother's milk." This is also the basis for the two sets of separate dishes and utensils which observers of the Dietary Laws use—one for "fleishig" (meat), the other for "milchig" (dairy).

It is also noteworthy that the word "kosher" is not con-

25

fined to foods. It has a broader application. Like a Scroll of the Law, other items are termed "kosher" when they are "ritually proper," pure, clean, and as required by Jewish law.

How Come That Some Jews Do, While Other Jews Do Not, Observe the Jewish Dietary Laws?

Jews who subscribe to the immutability of the Law, both Written (Pentateuch) and Oral (Talmud) are thus committed to the observance of the Dietary regulations. Their diet must be strictly "kosher." However, not all Jews subscribe to the aforementioned Traditionalist view of the Law and consequently do not feel themselves bound to observe the Dietary Laws.

Why Are Jews Such a Persecuted People?

This question smacks of an antiquated belief in divine retributive justice which conceives of "good for good" and "bad for bad." According to such thinking, the persecution of Jews throughout the ages must be proof of the punishment that fits the crime, God-sent suffering for Jewish sinfulness. This is the very point of view with which the Book of Job comes to grips and repudiates. The three friends contend that Job's misfortunes are manifestations of guilt and divine displeasure. But in the epilogue of the Book, God vindicates Job and condemns the friends' irrational

26

belief in such divine retributive justice. What is true of the individual holds good for a people. What persecution the Jewish people has suffered can neither be attributed to God nor punishment for sinfulness. To imply that the recent "liquidation" of six million Jews by the Nazis was the will of God would be an impeachment of His goodness, and to absolve the murderers of any guilt. It would be to accept any and all forms of persecution as divine intent, and absolve all persecutors. This is not reasonable.

Jacques Maritain, an eminent Catholic savant, in his letter to the International Council of Christians and Jews (printed in full in the Catholic journal, "Commonweal," for February 27, 1948) wrote, with reference to the six million murdered Jews, "For truly it was the 'chosen' quality of the Jews, truly it was Moses and the Prophets in the Jews, that the persecutors were persecuting. It was the savior who came from the Jewish people whom the persecutors hated." In other words, and according to this Christian's opinion, Jews have been persecuted for being the "Christ-bearers" rather than the charged "Christ-killers." Tyrants, dictators and bigots have found that the charge sticks and keeps the Jewish people vulnerable. They found that because of this, the Jewish minority was a convenient scapegoat when a scapegoat was needed. It was easy to use the Jew to divert attention from themselves, to blame him for everything that was wrong, and dupe the mobs and masses into joining in the persecution of defenseless Jews.

It is noteworthy that the Jewish people has also been called "the barometer of civilization" for the manner in which Jews are treated accurately registers the status of man's humanity or inhumanity to man.

II. JEWISH SOURCES

Is the Jewish Bible the Same as the Christian Bible?

The Christian Bible is the Jewish Bible plus the New Testament. Protestants and Catholics, in their versions of the Bible, have a different order of the "Books of the Old Testament"; the Catholics also include part of the Apocrypha, that part which they treat and term as "deuterocanonical." (See "Apocrypha," page 37.)

The terms "Old" and "New" Testaments do not apply to the Jewish Bible. There being no "New" Testament therein, there is no such divisional differentiation.

Christian use of the terms "Old" and "New" Testaments is clearly and ably explained by Dr. Samuel Sandmel in his book "A Jewish Understanding of the New Testament" on page 3, viz, "The word 'Testament' is to be understood in the sense of covenant. The Old Testament, which Jews call the Bible records a 'covenant' between God and Abraham, and Abraham's favored descendants, the Children of Israel. The New Covenant is the record of a similar compact between God and the new or 'true' descendants of Abraham, the Christian church. The title page of a recent translation, the American Standard Revised Version, published in 1946, begins: 'The New Covenant commonly called The New Testament . . .'

"The New is to be understood as a contrast, though not quite in opposition, to the Old Testament. The New is more recent and . . . tends for Christians, in some but not in all ways, to supplant and supersede the Old."

How Many Books Are There in the Bible?

In the Jewish Bible (known as the Old Testament) there are thirty-nine (39) books; in the Christian King James Version of the Bible, sixty-six (66)—thirty-nine (39) in the Old Testament and twenty-seven (27) in the New Testament; in the Catholic Douay-Rheims Version, seventy-three (73)—forty-six (46) in the Old Testament and twenty-seven (27) in the New Testament. The seven (7) additional books in the Catholic Version of the Old Testament are those called "deuterocanonical" by Catholics, while to Jews and Protestants they are known as belonging to the Apocrypha.

––––––––

What Does the Word "Bible" Mean?

The word "Bible" emerges from the Greek "biblia," the plural of "biblion," which means a collection of books. Hence, it should be noted that the Bible is not a book, but an anthology.

––––––––

When Was the Jewish Bible Written?

The Bible was written over many centuries, in different countries, and is the work of many men. The material was written over a period of about 1500 years, from about 1750 to 250 B.C.E.

What Are the Names of the Three Major Divisions of the Jewish Bible?

They are:
    a. *Torah,* the first Five Books, linked to Moses.
    b. *N'viim* (Prophets), comprising the books telling of the Early Prophets and the Later Prophets.
    c. *Ksuvim* (Writings) various literary works, such as Psalms, Proverbs, Ecclesiastes, Ezra, Chronicles, etc.; also known as Hagiographa or Holy Writings.

The initials of these three words form the term *Tanach,* by which the Bible is often known in Hebrew.

What Are the English and Hebrew Names of the First Five Books of the Bible?

The Hebrew names are often taken from the first verse of the book. The English names are sometimes more thematic in nature. The books are:
    a. Genesis, meaning Beginning. The Hebrew is *B'reshis* (In the beginning).
    b. Exodus, meaning Departure (from Egypt). The Hebrew is *Shmos* (Names).
    c. Leviticus, meaning Priestly. The Hebrew is *Vayikra* (And He called).
    d. Numbers, refers to the census taken of the Israelites. The Hebrew is *B'midbar* (In the desert).
    e. Deuteronomy, meaning Second Version, or Recapitulation, referring to the fact that Moses reviewed for the second generation of the desert what had happened

to their predecessors. The Hebrew is *D'vorim*
(Words).

What Is Meant by "Pentateuch"?

It is a term based upon the Greek *pentateuchos, penta*
meaning "five" and *teuchos* meaning "book." Pentateuch is
the term referring to the first five books of the Bible, col-
lectively. Hebrew equivalents are *Chumash* (five) and *Torah*
(The Teachings).

Where in the Bible Will You Find the Ten Commandments?

Exodus 20. 2-14 and Deuteronomy 5.6-18.

Where Does the Bible Urge You to Love Your Neighbor?

Leviticus 19.18 ". . . but thou shalt love thy neighbor
as thyself . . ." Note also 19.34, urging love of the stranger.

Who Are the Three Major Prophets?

They are Isaiah, Jeremiah and Ezekiel. They are called "major" not necessarily because they are the most important, but because we have more of their writings than the others. In Latin the word major means larger. There are twelve so-called later "minor" prophets.

———————

What Is Meant by "Torah"?

Torah is a Hebrew word derived from *yarah*, whose etymology has to do with shooting an arrow, and may best be translated as "moral teaching" (that which is aimed at one's mind and spirit). The word is frequently translated as "law," and Judaism has been described as a "religion of law." But this is a misconception, because the word Torah is instruction, as well as legislation. The word has several significations:

   a. The first five books of the Bible, associated with Moses, is known as *Toras Moshe* (*Toras*—the teaching of, *Moshe*—Moses).
   b. The Scroll on which the first five books of the Bible are written and from which they are read on Sabbaths and Festivals is also known as the Torah.
   c. Learning in general is designated as Torah. A Jewish religious school is referred to as a Talmud Torah (the study of Torah).

What Are Megillos?

The word *Megillos* is the plural of *Megillah,* meaning a "roll" or "scroll." There are five books in the Bible referred to as "The Five Megillos." They are: Song of Songs (read on Passover), Ruth (Shovous), Lamentations (Ninth of Av), Ecclesiastes (Sukos) and Esther (Purim).

Which Three Biblical Books Are Traditionally Attributed to Solomon?

They are The Song of Songs (which the Pharisees claimed that he wrote when he was young); Proverbs, reflecting Solomon's great wisdom in his adult years; and Ecclesiastes, said to reflect the cynicism of his old age. (Some of the psalms in The Book of Psalms are also traditionally attributed to Solomon).

Did the Miracles in the Bible Really Happen?

One who interprets the Bible literally and regards it as infallible, answers "Yes." The answer is also "Yes" according to the Talmud. Those who view the Bible more critically interpret some of the miracles as natural phenomena, interpret others as dramatizations, by human writers, of the great blessings bestowed by God.

In a pre-scientific age, the Biblical miracles were accepted as true. They were needed to reinforce faith. Today, however, modernists find evidence in other terms, such as the order of the cosmos, the wonder of creation, et cetera.

What Is the Apocrypha?

The Apocrypha, from the Greek *"apokryphos"* meaning "hidden," is (or, properly, are) a collection of religious books written after the Bible (Old Testament) was completed and canonized. (It is generally accepted that the canon of the Old Testament was closed about 250 B.C.E. and received final rabbinical ratification at Jamnia, Palestine, in 90 C.E.) The term "Apocrypha" was applied to this non-canonical collection of books, written sometime between 200 B.C.E. and 100 C.E., when prophecy and direct revelation were believed to be no more. They were "hidden away" and "kept secret" because of doubtful authority and authorship, and because they were considered to contain "a mysterious and esoteric wisdom" for the select and not for the masses, a wisdom requiring knowledge and intelligence for comprehension.

While the Apocrypha is outside of the Jewish Bible and the Protestant Bible based upon it, the Catholic Church at its Council of Trent (16th Century C.E.) affirmed the canonicity of many of the books and includes them in their Bible as "deuterocanonical."

The names and order of the Books called "Apocrypha" are: I Esdras; II Esdras; Tobit; Judith; The Rest of Esther; The Wisdom of Solomon; Ecclesiasticus (also: The Wisdom of Jesus, the Son of Sirach); Baruch, with the Epistle of Jeremiah; The Song of the Three Holy Children; The History of Susanna; Bel and the Dragon; The Prayer of Manasses; I Maccabees; and II Maccabees. These (with the exception of I, II Esdras and The Prayer of Manasses) are called "deuterocanonical" by Catholics and are included in their versions of the Old Testament.

What Is the Mishnah?

The word *Mishnah* comes from the Hebrew *Shanah* meaning "repeat"—to teach or learn by means of repetition. The term Mishnah is applied to a body of religious writing which prior to their being collected and put into writing were circulated in Jewish life by oral transmission. These commentaries on the Bible constituted efforts to interpret the Bible for the regulation of Jewish life in the light of changing conditions and circumstances. The collection spans four centuries, beginning in the first half of the second century B.C.E. and gathered, edited and composed in its final edition by Rabbi Judah Ha-Nasi and his disciples by 220 C.E.

What Is Pirke Ovos?

A tractate of the Mishnah, "The Chapters of the Fathers," is a collection of the sayings handed down in the name of sixty sages who lived between 300 B.C.E. and 200 C.E., from Simon the Just to Rabbi Judah Ha-Nasi, the editor of the Mishnah. Sometimes the tractate is called, "The Ethics of the Fathers."

Here are some typical sayings from Pirke Ovos:

"The world rests upon three things: upon the Torah, upon worship, and upon acts of kindness." (Chapter I, verse 2).

Said Ben Zoma: "Who is wise? He who learns from everybody . . . Who is mighty? He who subdues his passions . . . Who is rich? He who rejoices in his portion . . . Who is worthy of honor? He who honors his fellowmen . . ." (Chapter IV, verse 1).

* * *

"There are seven marks of an uncultured, and seven of a wise man. The wise man does not speak before him who is greater than he in wisdom; and does not break in upon the speech of his fellow; he is not hasty to answer; he questions according to the subject matter, and answers to the point; he speaks upon the first thing first, and the last last; regarding that which he has not understood he says, I do not understand it; and he acknowledges the truth. The reverse of all this is to be found in an uncultured man." (Chapter V, verse 10).

What Is the Talmud?

The word *Talmud* comes from the Hebrew *lomad* meaning "learn" or "study." The term Talmud designates a further collection of interpretations of the Bible, actually commentaries on the Mishnah. These commentaries are known as *Gemara* (*gemar*—finish). There are two Gemaras; one grew up in Palestine, the other in Babylonia. Mishnah and Gemara constitute the Talmud. It contains discussions and elaborations on Judaism.

There are two Talmuds: the *Yerushalmi* (Jerusalem or Palestinian) made up of the Mishnah and Palestinian Ge-

39

mara, and the *Babli* (Babylonian) consisting of the Mishnah and Babylonian Gemara. The former was completed about 400 C.E.; the latter, about 500 C.E. The *Babli* is the larger and more consulted work and is commonly referred to as The Talmud.

What Is the Midrash?

Midrash (from *darash*, literally, searching out, exploration, or explanation; plural, *midrashim*) are homilies and illustrative material based upon applications of Biblical ideas to life in general. The term in its broadest sense has reference to Hebrew Scriptural exegesis made during a period of about 1500 years after the Exile (586 B.C.E.), largely based upon tradition, and represented by the two types: *Haggada* (moral lessons, ethical teachings) and *Halacha* (practice or rule, pure religious practice and legal matters). When Midrash is used without specification, its reference is commonly to the former.

Part of the Talmud comprises narratives and case studies which might be designated as Midrashic. The word Midrash has also come, in rabbinical circles, to be used to designate far-fetched ideas, inasmuch as occasionally the Midrashists allowed considerable play to their fantasies.

What Is the Zohar?

The Hebrew word "Zohar" means "shining" or "brilliance." It is the name of the basic book of Jewish Cabalism. Its authorship and date of composition are uncertain. A Talmudic story claims it for the reputed miracle-working Rabbi Simeon ben Yohai who lived in Palestine in the second century of the Common Era. Some believed it to be the work of one Moses de Leon, who lived in Granada, Spain, in the thirteenth century. But neither claim is convincingly substantiated. The consensus of modern scholarship is that the book is not the work of a single author, or of a single period, but the creation of many hands, a "compilation of a mass of material drawn from many strata of Jewish and non-Jewish mystical thought and covering numerous centuries . . . much of it dating back to the early centuries before and after the destruction of the Second Temple (70 C.E.) ."

Under the form of a running commentary of the Pentateuch, written partly in Aramaic and partly in Hebrew, the Zohar includes many Talmudic teachings and mystical speculations on God, Torah and the universe. It deals with the mysteries of creation, the human soul, the relation between spirit and matter, good and evil, angelology and demonology, astrology and magic, paradise and hell, et cetera. It interprets the Bible allegorically and by means of "gematria," a Cabalistic method of trying to ferret out hidden meanings in Hebrew letters, words, vowel-points and numbers.

Even though Judaism is essentially rationalistic, the Zohar has had a pronounced, though peripheral effect upon the Jewish prayerbook ideologically and phraseologically, as well as an acknowledged marked influence upon Christian mysticism.

41

III. HOLY DAYS AND HOLIDAYS

The Jewish Calendar Is a Lunar Calendar. What Does That Mean?

Actually the Jewish calendar is a lunar-solar calendar. This means that it is based upon the movements of the moon, with certain modifications based upon the sun. The solar adjustments are necessary for Passover—the Spring Festival, Shovuos—the Summer Festival, and Sukos—the Autumn Festival, to be in season.

Since the lunar month numbers about 29.53 days, and the lunar year about 354⅓ days, the average lunar year is shorter than the solar one by 10-plus days. To make up for the difference in the accumulated shortage and to take care of the necessary seasonal adjustments, a leap month is added every two or three years. In the cycle of nineteen years, the third, sixth, eighth, eleventh, fourteenth, seventeenth and nineteenth are leap-years; the rest are common years. The lunar leap-year with thirteen instead of twelve months, 383-plus days instead of 354⅓ days, takes care of the calendarial adjustments.

The lunar-solar feature of the Jewish calendar also explains why Jewish holidays do not always occur on the exact solar Gregorian calendar date, but vary.

It is also noteworthy that the ecclesiastical calendar used by the Christian Church for regulating the dates of church feasts (i.e. Easter) , as well as the calendar of the Mohammedans, are lunisolar.

45

There Are Certain Jewish Holidays to Which Orthodox and Conservative Jews Add an Extra Day. Which and Why?

Rosh Hashonah two days instead of one; Sukos eight days instead of seven; Passover eight days instead of seven; and Shovuos two days instead of one. In a lunar-solar calendar, such as is the Jewish calendar, the months are according to the appearance of the new moon. Before there was a fixed calendar there was uncertainty whether the new month was to begin after the 29th or 30th day. In Palestine the new month was announced when the new moon became visible. If it was not seen as expected, a second day was added to the holidays of that month to insure their being observed on the correct day and in accordance with Biblical prescription. Outside of Palestine, the rabbis had no jurisdiction over the calendar, so they adopted the custom of observing the second day whether the new moon appeared as expected or not. This custom became tradition and even after the establishment of the fixed Jewish calendar the extra days continued to be added outside of Palestine.

In the State of Israel today the only extra day added is to Rosh Hashonah and even so it is traditionally viewed as one "long day," by the "extension" of the extra day. All other Holy Days and Festivals are there observed as stipulated in the Bible (i.e. minus the extra day).

Reform Judaism, because of the mathematical precision with which the established calendar was fixed, sees no need for, and does not add any extra days to any Jewish holidays, but observes the number set forth in the Bible.

What Is Rosh Hashonah?

Rosh—"head" or "beginning" of; Hashonah—"the year." The Jewish New Year marks the beginning of a ten-day period of spiritual renewal known as the Jewish High Holy Days. Unconnected with any historic event or personage, Rosh Hashonah is marked by Worship Services, prayers for divine forgiveness for one's shortcomings, the sounding of the Shofar, or ram's horn, as a call to conscience in Temple and Synagogue, and resolutions to help create a better life for oneself and one's fellowmen. Rosh Hashonah comes on the first day of the month of Tishri, the seventh month of the Jewish calendar.

Actually and according to the Bible, the Israelites had two separate and distinct beginnings of the year. As G. A. Barrois (*Interpreter's Bible I*, page 152) points out: "The first day of Nisan (in the spring) marks the beginning of the year with regard to the computation of Passover. For other purposes the year began in autumn, on the first of Tishri, which was solemnized as New Year's day." Some, today, explain the former, the month of the exodus from Egypt, as the beginning of the political New Year; the latter, the first of the seventh month (seven, the most sacred Jewish number enhanced by the institution of the Sabbath) the beginning of the spiritual New Year.

There is also the New Year of the Trees. (See Chamisho Osor Bi-sh'vot page 54.)

What Is a Shofar?

A Shofar is a ram's horn. It is sounded in temple and synagogue on Rosh Hashonah (the Jewish New Year) as a call to conscience, in accordance with the Biblical prescription contained in Leviticus 23.24 and Numbers 29.1. The blast on Rosh Hashonah is to put the Jewish people in mind of the Akeda story, Genesis 22, when Abraham was summoned to sacrifice his son Isaac and a ram was substituted in the final moments for his son. We are thus summoned to emulate the complete faith displayed at that time by the first patriarch. The blast of the Shofar is also intended to penetrate the human soul to arouse it from its lethargy to renewed spiritual life. It concludes the Yom Kippur Service, too.

What Is Shabbas Shuva?

The Sabbath of Repentance, which comes during the Ten Penetential Days between Rosh Hashonah and Yom Kippur. The word "Shuva" (literally, "return") is the opening word in the prophetical portion, Hosea 14.2, which Jewish tradition has assigned for reading on this particular Sabbath. The Prophet's call is "Return, O Israel, unto the Lord, thy God . . ."

What Is Yom Kippur?

Yom—day of; Kippur—atonement, the holiest day in the Jewish calendar, is the final day of the High Holy Days, the tenth day of the month of Tishri. The Day of Atonement is devoted to fasting, meditation, prayer, repentance, reconciliation with man and God, and worship directed towards realizing the potential for goodness which God has deposited within the human spirit. See Book of Leviticus, Chapter 23.27; and Book of Numbers 29.7.

———

What Are the Names of the Three Pilgrim Festivals?

Sukos, or Tabernacles, the Autumn Festival; Pesach or Passover, the Spring Festival; and Shovuos, or Pentecost, the Summer Festival. All were originally associated with milestones in the life of the Jewish farmer who would thank God for His bounty and would travel to the ancient Temple at Jerusalem to offer prayers and sacrifices on Sukos in thanksgiving for the harvest, and on Pesach and Shovuos in petition for a prosperous year. See Book of Deuteronomy, 16.16.

———

What Is Sukos?

Sukos is the Feast of Tabernacles, the Jewish Harvest Festival, biblically enjoined in the Book of Leviticus, Chapter 23. It begins on the fifteenth day of the Jewish month of Tishri and lasts "for seven days" and an octave. Orthodox

49

and Conservative Jews living outside of the Holy Land observe an added ninth day (see "Extra Day" page 46). Its observance calls for the following accompanying symbols, "the fruit of goodly trees" (represented by the *Esrog*); "branches of palm-trees, and boughs of thick trees, and willows of the brook" (featured with the *Lulav*); and the *Sukah,* the booth. Consecrated time, Sukos strikes the chords of Jewish memory recalling the wilderness trek when God "made the children of Israel to dwell in booths, when (He) brought them out of the land of Egypt" en route to the Promised Land. The "fruits of the land" which adorn the sukah, as symbols of the harvest, prompt thoughts of divine providence and thanksgiving.

It was from Sukos that the Pilgrims took inspiration for the American Festival of Thanksgiving.

What Is a Sukah?

A hut or booth covered with green branches, the inside of which is decorated with various fruits and vegetables. According to Leviticus 23.43, and in connection with the Feast of Tabernacles, it is to serve as a reminder of the booths in which the children of Israel dwelt after leaving Egypt. The fruits and vegetables with which it is adorned are symbolic of the harvest aspect of Sukos (Deuteronomy 16.13-15).

50

What Are "Lulav" and "Esrog"?

The *Lulav* and *Esrog* constitute the group of the Four Species mentioned in connection with the observance of Sukos in Leviticus 23.40. The *Lulav* combines three of the species in an arrangement in which a triple holder of braided palm leaves supports the *Lulav* (a branch of a palm tree) in the center, the *Hadassah* (myrtle branch) to its right, and the *Aravah* (willow branch) to its left. The *Esrog* is a citron, whose fragrance represents the pleasant effect of good deeds.

What Is Simchas Torah?

Literally, "Rejoicing over the Torah," it is a gay holiday which follows immediately upon Sukos, the Autumn Festival. On that day, the reading of the Torah cycle is completed, and, in Temple and Synagogue, the reading of the last verses of the Book of Deuteronomy is followed immediately by the reading of the first few verses of the Book of Genesis, to dramatize the continuity of study and devotion to the moral law. The holiday is marked also by festivity, processions of the Torahs in Temple and Synagogue, children carrying flags, and special songs and prayers of a jubilant character. The term "Hakkofos" (plural of the Hebrew "Hakkafah" meaning "going around" or "circuit") is applied to the sevenfold processional during which the Scrolls of the Law are carried seven times around the sanctuary. To receive a "Hakkafah," is to be honored with the privilege of carrying a Scroll in one of the processions.

51

What Is Passover?

Passover, or Pesach, is the Jewish Spring Festival, which in its earliest form was an agricultural celebration of Spring's arrival. One of the meanings of the Hebrew word "pesach" is "skipping over." Applied to the festival it envisions the friskiness of the lambs of the Israelite shepherds at the arrival of Spring.

In time, however, Pesach was appropriated to commemorate the deliverance of the Israelites from Egyptian slavery. The word "pesach" was associated with the Exodus account of the tenth and final plague when the Angel of Death "passed over" the houses of the Children of Israel, when he smote the Egyptians. Passover came to be regarded as the springtime of Jewish history. Just as Spring liberates nature from Winter, so Passover was the springtime deliverance and emergence of the Children of Israel from the grip of slavery.

Since that distant day, Jews have observed the Feast of Passover as ordained in the Book of Exodus, Chapter 13. The holiday begins on the fifteenth day of the month of Nisan and lasts for "seven days." Orthodox and Conservative Jews living outside of the Holy Land observe an added eighth day. The Passover meal, or Seder, ushers in the Holiday on the evening of the first day (Orthodox and Conservative Jews hold Seders on the evenings of the first two days), and is conducted according to the Haggadah.

The word *Haggadah* comes from the Hebrew, meaning "to tell." This book, more fully called "Haggadah Shel Pesach" contains the narrative of the Passover in the ritual provided for the Seder home-service.

Matzo (plural, matzos) or unleavened bread is eaten throughout the Passover season commemorating the haste

52

with which the Israelites fled Egypt and had no time to leaven their bread.

What Is Shovuos?

Seven weeks after the beginning of Passover, on the sixth day of the Jewish month of Sivan, comes "Shovuos" (Hebrew for "weeks"), "The Festival of Weeks," so called because of the seven weeks interval. Ordained in Scriptures as a time to give thanks for the beginning of the summer harvest, the holiday is also known as "the feast of harvest" (Exodus 23.16), "the day of the first-fruits" (Numbers 28.26), and "Pentecost" (the Greek for "fiftieth day") because it is celebrated on the fiftieth day (seven weeks) after the second day of Passover. It is a one-day observance. However, Orthodox and Conservative Jews living outside of the Holy Land add a second day (see "Extra Day" page 46).

According to Jewish tradition, the revelation of Mt. Sinai took place on Shovuos. Hence, the festival is also designated as the birthday of the Ten Commandments. Since on the first Shovuos, the Children of Israel avowed the need for moral purposes in their daily living, Reform Judaism has introduced the ceremony of Confirmation into its Temples on this holiday.

What Is Chanukah?

The word "Chanukah" means "dedication" or "re-dedication." It is the name of a Jewish holiday.

About 165 years before the Christian era the ruler of that part of the world which included Judea sought to impose idolatry upon the Jews. The latter resisted the plan of the Syrian-Grecian ruler, Antiochus by name, and the result was a three-year war, history's first struggle for religious freedom. Despite overwhelming odds the Judeans were successful and joyously engaged in the re-dedication (Chanukah) of their Temple which the pagans had desecrated.

The struggle is commemorated annually by Jews for eight days, kindling candles, singing songs, exchanging gifts, offering prayers of thanksgiving, and rededicating themselves to the cause of religious liberty in their Chanukah celebrations.

Traditionally a minor holiday, Chanukah has gained in popularity and observance in recent years. Indeed, it receives more attention in homes and religious schools than many a holiday traditionally deemed more sacred.

————

What Is Chamisho Osor Bi-sh'vot?

Chamisho (five), *Osor* (ten) and *Bi-Sh'vot* (in Sh'vot) is the fifteenth day of the Jewish month of *Sh'vot*, the New Year of the trees according to the Mishnah—Jewish Arbor Day. It is also known as "Tu Bi-Sh'vot"; "tu" being the two Hebrew letters which signify 9 and 6: 15.

This holiday is today, in the main, celebrated outside of the State of Israel, by purchasing trees to be planted there. Many also relish the custom of eating "bokser," the sweetish long pods of the carob tree found in the Mediterranean region. The fruit of this tree is also known as "St.-John's-bread." Israeli Jews mark the day with plantings and gaieties of the season.

––––––––––

What Is Purim?

The name of the Jewish holiday called Purim comes from the Hebrew word "Pur" meaning "lot"; the plural, "Purim."

As recounted in the Biblical Book of Esther, Haman, a Persian vizier, demanded that all men bow down to him. All did, apparently, except Mordecai. Angered, Haman decided to eliminate not only Mordecai but all of his fellow-Jews. His plot was thwarted by Mordecai who prevailed upon Esther, the girl who became the bride of the king, to intercede with King Ahasuerus on behalf of the Jewish people. To celebrate the deliverance, Jews annually celebrate the holiday of Purim (so called because Haman determined the date of his near-pogrom by means of "lots") by re-reading the Book of Esther, giving gifts to the poor, offering prayers and songs of thanksgiving, and rededicating themselves to the belief in human freedom.

––––––––––

What Commandment Is the Basis for the Sabbath?

The basis for the observance of the Jewish Sabbath is the Fourth Commandment (Exodus 20.18-11 and Deuteronomy 5.12-15). It begins at Friday sundown, the beginning of the seventh day, the Sabbath, according to the Jewish lunar-solar calendar.

————

How Should the Sabbath Be Observed?

In the home, the Sabbath Eve table should be set in a manner befitting the Sabbath. Candles should be kindled with the recitation of the appropriate blessing by mother and daughters. *Kiddush* ("sanctification," to make holy), the blessing over the wine should be recited or chanted by the male head of the household over the cup of wine. Wine is to symbolize happiness and is linked with the thought expressed in Psalm 104.15. "And wine that maketh glad the heart of man." The *Motzi* prayer should be recited by all in unison before partaking of the *Challah,* the special braided loaf of bread for the Sabbath. The Sabbath should also be observed by attending worship services, some study, some recreation, some meditation, and deeds which differ from the week's routine.

The appropriate blessings for the candles, *kiddush* and *motzi* follow.

OVER THE CANDLES

BORUCH ATTO ADONOI ELOHENU MELECH
HO'OLOM ASHER KIDD'SHONU B'MITZVOSOV
V'TZIVONU L'HADLIK NER SHEL SHABBOS.
(on festivals add: V'YOM TOV).
Blessed art Thou, O Lord, our God, King of the universe,
Who hast sanctified us by Thy commandments, and has

56

commanded us to kindle the Sabbath lights (on festivals: "Sabbath and Festival lights)."

OVER THE WINE

BORUCH ATTO ADONOI ELOHENU MELECH HO'OLOM BORE P'RI HAGGOFEN.
Praised art Thou, O Lord our God, Ruler of the world, Who hast created the fruit of the vine.

OVER THE BREAD

BORUCH ATTO ADONOI ELOHENU MELECH HO'OLOM HAMOTZI LECHEM MIN HO'ORETZ.
Blessed Art Thou, O Lord our God, King of the universe, Who bringest forth bread from the earth.

What Does "Oneg Shabbat" Mean?

Oneg—pleasure of; *Shabbat*—Sabbath. It is also translated as "Spiritual joy of the Sabbath." The term is applied to gatherings and special pleasures to be enjoyed in honor of, and in connection with, the Sabbath. Plural: *Ongay Shabbat.*

What Is a B'somim (Spice) Box Used For?

As part of the *Havdalah* (Separation) Ceremony on Saturday night, a ceremony to distinguish between the Sabbath and the midweek. A blessing is chanted over the spices in the B'somim box. The fragrance of the spices is to delight "the yearning spirit at the moment when the beloved Sabbath is departing." Some interpret it to symbolize the hope for "a fragrant week ahead."

————

IV. IN TEMPLE AND SYNAGOGUE

Is There Any Difference Between a "Temple" and a "Synagogue"?

Technically, yes. Traditionalist Jews reserve the term, "temple" (Latin: "holy place"), for the ancient shrine in Jerusalem which, they believe, will be restored in the days of the Messiah. Reform Judaism, having abandoned this belief as well as the belief in a personal Messiah, designated its houses of worship as "temples" to signify that they were successors of the Temple of old. Traditionalist Jews who reserve the term "Temple" for the Jerusalem shrine accordingly incline to designate their houses of worship as "synagogues" (Greek: "meeting houses"). However, there are those who use the terms "temple" and "synagogue" interchangeably, for in function they are essentially the same. Each serves as a "Beth Ha-tifilah—House of Prayer," "Beth Ha-Midrash—House of Study," and "Beth Ha-keneset —House of Assembly."

What Is the Meaning of "Aron Ha-kodesh"?

Aron (ark of) *Ha-Kodesh* (the holiness), is the name for the Ark which contains the Scrolls of the Torah in every Jewish house of worship.

First mention of such an Ark is contained in the Book of Exodus 25.10,16 (God orders Moses to have the children of Israel "make an ark of acacia-wood" for "the testimony.") ; and in Exodus 37.1 ("And Bezalel made the ark of acacia-wood . . .").

In the Temple in Jerusalem the Ark was called the "Holy of Holies" and symbolized the dwelling place of God. Its place in that shrine accounts for its presence and centrality in every Jewish house of worship. In addition to symbolizing the Divine Presence, it is the repository for the Scrolls of the Torah which bear the words of God.

––––––––

What Is the Meaning of "Sefer Torah"?

Sefer means "Book of," and *Torah* represents the First Five Books of the Bible. The *Sefer Torah* is Hebrew for the parchment Scroll containing the Pentateuch.

The plural of *Sefer Torah* is *Sifre Torah*.

––––––––

What Is a Yod?

Literally, "a hand." It refers to the pointer with which the Torah is read. It is to prevent finger soiling of the parchment or possible gradual erasure of some part of the text or finger perspiration smearing and thus obscuring some letter or word. To do so, the rabbis considered a violation of the prohibition in Deuteronomy 4.2, "Ye shall not add unto the word which I command you, neither shall ye diminish from it . . ." So the Yod was conceived and introduced as a preventative.

What Is Meant by "Sidra" and "Parashah"?

Sidra, meaning "order" or "arrangement" is the term used to designate the weekly Pentateuchal portion read in Temple and Synagogue. There are two orders or arrangements of these Scriptural readings; one according to an annual cycle, the other according to a triennial one. The weekly Sidrot (plural) are read in order beginning with "Bereshis (In the Beginning)," "Noah," "Lech Lecho (Go thou)," et cetera. Special Scriptural readings are assigned to Holy Days and Festivals, readings germane to the occasion.

The term "Parashah" (plural: Parashiyyot) used by Sephardic Jews is synonymous with "Sidra" (plural: Sidrot), the Ashkenazic term.

It is noteworthy that the Jewish calendar which has no names for the days of the week other than "Sabbath" for the seventh day, does give to each week the name of its Sidra (or Parashah).

What Is Meant by "Haftarah"?

Literally, "conclusion," "leave" or "to take leave," this term is applied to the Prophetical passage which accompanies and is read following the Pentateuchal portion at Worship Services. A sort of appendix to the reading, it has been pictured as "the means by which we (conclude) or take leave of the Scriptures for the time being."

The exact origin of this custom is unknown. While Talmudic sources trace the custom of reading the Torah (Pentateuch) to Moses and Ezra (i.e. Deuteronomy 1.5 and Nehemiah 8.2-3), there are no such references to the initial readings of the Haftarah.

Some scholars incline to believe that portions of the Prophetical Books, once they were compiled and edited, were added to the Pentateuchal reading in order to emphasize the former's sacred character and part of Holy Writ.

The Jewish Encyclopedia (Volume VI, page 136) calls attention to "Abudarham, a Spanish teacher of the fourteenth century, (who) traces the Haftarah back to the time of the persecution under Antiocus IV, Epiphanes (168-165 B.C.), when, owing to the prohibition against reading from the Torah, the corresponding sections from the Prophets were read instead, this practice becoming established as a custom."

What Is Meant by "Maftir"?

Maftir from the Hebrew meaning "to dismiss" or "discharge" is the term applied to the reader who concludes the reading from the Torah (Pentateuch) portion followed by his reading of the Haftarah (Prophetical) portion.

Where there is a Bar Mitzvah, this privilege and honor are accorded to him.

What Is the Meaning of "Ner Tomid"?

Ner Tomid is Hebrew for "Eternal Light," referring to the lamp to be seen over the Ark in every Jewish House of Worship. Its everlasting illumination is a symbol of, among other things, God's never-ending beneficence. See Leviticus 24.2-4.

What Is the Meaning of "Siddur"?

Siddur is a derivative of the Hebrew *Seder*—Order. It is the term applied to the traditional prayerbook which contains all daily and weekly prayers. The term is applied, in the main, to prayerbooks used by Orthodox and Conservative Jews.

What Is the Meaning of "Mahzor"?

Mahzor is a derivative of the Hebrew *hazar*—"to repeat" or to "go around," and has reference to the "cycle" of Piyutim (Aramaic inclusive term for all kinds of synagogal poetry) for the holidays. The term Mahzor is applied to prayerbooks containing the ritual for High Holy Days and major festivals. The Mahzor as used by Orthodox Jewish congregations is usually arranged in two volumes. One volume contains the prayers for Rosh Hashonah and Yom Kippur; the other, the ritual for Passover, Sukos and Shovuos.

The Reform equivalent of the Mahzor is Volume II of the Union Prayerbook.

Who Wrote the Union Prayerbook?

The Union Prayerbook is the prayerbook of Reform Judaism, in two volumes. It is based upon the traditional Siddur and Mahzor and contains in addition a composite of passages from the Bible, from the Siddur, from Hebrew classics and the writings of contemporary rabbis. Or it might be described as a modified version of the traditional prayerbook, omitting much old and including much new material. The Union Prayerbook is edited and published by the Central Conference of American Rabbis.

What Is Meant by "T'hilim"?

Psalms or the Book of Psalms, from the Hebrew *tehillah*, meaning adoration or song of praise.

What Does "Ayn Kelohaynoo" Mean?

"*Ayn*" is the Hebrew word meaning "there is none;" "*Kelohaynoo*" means "like our God." They are the initial words of the traditional hymn, "Ayn Kelohaynoo (There is none like our God)."

V. LIFE CYCLE CEREMONIES

What Is "Bris Milah"?

What Is the Significance of Circumcision to the Jewish People?

The ceremony of circumcision which takes place for the male Jewish infant on the eighth day after birth, initiates him into the Covenant of Abraham, as recorded in Scriptures (Genesis 17.10 ff). Circumcision serves as the token of the covenant between God and the male descendants of Abraham. The rite, ordained to take place on the eighth day after birth, is neither to be preponed nor postponed. If the eighth day happens to be a Sabbath or even the Day of Atonement, the circumcision is held thereon. Postponement is permitted *only* because of the illness of the child or mother.

The circumcision is performed by either a Mohel (Hebrew for "circumciser") or a surgeon. Where a Mohel officiates, he will do both the operation and recite the accompanying prayers. When a surgeon performs the circumcision, a Rabbi reads the service.

The ritual includes the giving of the name to the infant. (Girls are traditionally named in the synagogue on the Sabbath following birth.)

Orthodox and Conservative Judaism also require circumcision of proselytes for admission into Judaism. Reform Judaism does not require this initiatory rite.

What Is Pidyon Ha-ben?

What Is the Ceremony About "Redeeming" Jewish Children?

It was an ancient practice that the first-born male child was to become a priest (*cohen*) or an assistant priest (*levi*). Parents who did not want their son to enter the service of the Temple could "redeem" him through a ceremony which came to be known as *pidyon* (redemption of) *ha-ben* (the son). The ceremony is marked by the payment of a small sum to a *cohen* or *levi,* which he turns over to charity, in remission of the obligation. Since Reform Judaism has discarded the whole notion about the importance of remembering the descendants of the priests (who, according to Orthodoxy, must stand ready to resume their duties when the Messiah comes), it has abandoned pidyon ha-ben. It is also widely disregarded by traditionalist Jews, although it is enjoying somewhat of a revival, not for religious reasons, but as an occasion for celebrating the birth of the baby. The ceremony is supposed to occur 30 days after the baby is born. (See Exodus 13.2, 12 and Numbers 18.15-16).

What Is Consecration?

It is a ceremony inducting youngsters into the Religious School. The ceremony, created by Reform Judaism, usually takes place in the temple on Simchas Torah, the holiday of "The Rejoicing over the Torah," which the children will study.

What Is a Bar Mitzvah?

Bar Mitzvah may be translated as "Son of Duty." Traditionally it marked a lad's attainment of religious majority at the age of 13. Therewith he assumed the obligation and responsibility for religious duties. As a religious major he numbers in a religious quorum.

Today, the rite of Bar Mitzvah is primarily a means to mark the completion of one stage of religious education, to strengthen Jewish allegiance, and to encourage mature religious attitudes in the teenager. The Bar Mitzvah is called to the Torah on the Sabbath following his thirteenth birthday, recites the benedictions, reads the weekly Torah and Prophetical portions, and may conclude with a short speech or prayer.

————

What Are "T'filin" or Phylacteries?

Two leather boxes to which are affixed thin loops which are bound around the arm and head in set fashion, in accordance with the Biblical injunction to keep the teachings of God ever before one as "a sign upon thy hand, and for frontlets between thine eyes" (Exodus 13.16). Four Biblical passages (Exodus 13.1-10 and Exodus 13.11-16, and Deuteronomy 6.4-9 and 11.13-21) each inscribed on four separate pieces of parchment are deposited in the four compartments of the head-box. The hand-box has only one compartment which contains one parchment sheet inscribed with the same four Biblical passages.

Beginning with Bar Mitzvah, devoutly Orthodox Jews put on their t'filin each morning except Saturday.

What Is a Bas Mitzvah?

It is a recent innovation, fashioned after Bar Mitzvah, for girls on the attainment of their thirteenth birthday. It is not as widely accepted by Jewish congregations as is Bar Mitzvah.

What Is Confirmation?

Confirmation is a religious ceremony generally held on Shovuos, which traditionally commemorates the giving of the Torah, when boys and girls at the completion of their elementary religious school training are confirmed in their faith. The Service is a solemn one in which the confirmand's understanding of, and attachment to, the precepts and practices of Judaism are indirectly, but nonetheless clearly, revealed. The ceremony enables young people to confirm what their ancestors affirmed at Sinai—fealty to Divine Mandates.

What Is the Significance of Breaking a Glass at a Jewish Wedding?

There are several explanations for this custom, which have been discarded by many Reform Jews. Actually, no one is certain of the origin or real purport of the practice. It was believed by some Jews that the breaking of the glass was to frighten away the evil spirits with which the superstitious populate the air. Another interpretation is that it reminds us, in the midst of great joy, of the fact that the ancient Temple lies in ruins. By extension, then, the glass-breaking is supposed to offset revelry with reverie of how we can use our happiness to add to the happiness of others.

Does Judaism Insist Upon a Religious as Well as a Civil Divorce?

Reform Judaism, no; traditionalist Judaism, yes. The latter requires that a Get, a Jewish "bill of divorce": (See Deuteronomy 24.1-4) be secured through the proper Jewish religious authorities after a civil divorce has been granted. Orthodox and Conservative rabbis will not officiate at the wedding of a couple where one or both parties, if formerly divorced, lack a Get. Reform rabbis do not require a religious divorce. They base their position upon the traditional Jewish principle of *"dina d'malchusa dina,"* namely that "the law of the land is the law." This is to say that the law of the land, the civil law, is binding on the Jewish people. Since a civil divorce is the prerequisite for the dissolution of a marriage, Reform rabbis honor such and do not insist upon a religious one as well.

What Does "Shiva" Mean?

Shivah is the Hebrew word for seven. The term is applied to the seven-day period of mourning which Jews traditionally observe beginning the day of burial for the following seven next of kin: father, mother, son, daughter, brother, sister, wife or husband.

What Is the Meaning of "Kaddish"?

The word means sanctification. It specifies the mourner's prayer of glorification of God, recited to thank Him for the loved ones whom in His abundant goodness He gave to us and in His infinite wisdom has seen fit to take away. The prayer seeks to reconcile the mourner with God's will and to strengthen fidelity to Him.

Actually containing no mention of death, the Kaddish prayer also serves as a punctuation between various segments of the order of Worship Service.

What Is the Meaning of "Yahrzeit"?

It is the Judeo-German term applied to the anniversary of the death of next of kin for whom one mourns.

On that day a Yahrzeit light is kindled which burns for twenty-four hours. It is linked with the thought expressed in Proverbs 20.27: "The spirit of man is the lamp of the Lord."

What Is Meant by "Yizkor"?

Yizkor is the first word of a prayer memorializing the dead. This prayer which begins "May He remember . . ." is part of the Memorial Service liturgy.

What Is Expected Religiously of Mourners?

Traditionally, they are supposed to observe the various periods of mourning:

Shivah (seven), following the funeral to kindle a seven-day lamp which is kept burning throughout the Shivah period; to remain at home for seven days after the funeral, with allowance to work after the third day where necessary; to hold daily Services in the house of mourning or to attend such at Temple or Synagogue; on Sabbaths and Festivals such services are not held, but the mourners attend worship services at Temple or Synagogue.

Sheloshim (thirty) days, during the first thirty days after the funeral to abstain from festivities and amusements (other prohibitions considered obligatory upon Orthodox Jews).

Eleven to twelve months, during this period the mourner, according to traditional Judaism, is expected to attend daily Services to recite the Kaddish, while Reform Jews are expected to attend the Sabbath Services throughout this period and to rise for the recitation of the Kaddish. Mourners are expected to see to it that a tombstone is placed upon the grave of the departed and properly dedicated.

A *Yahrzeit* candle is to be kindled in the home of the mourner in memory of the departed on the Yahrzeit, the anniversary of his or her passing. Attendance at a Worship Service on that day and rising for the recitation of the Kaddish is traditional. Where the mourner is a member of a Reform Temple and daily Services are not held, the anniversary of the passing of one's beloved may be commemorated at the Sabbath Service prior to, or following, the actual Yahrzeit date.

Those who are bereaved are expected to attend annually *Yizkor* (Memorial) Services whenever held in their Temple or Synagogue.

Why Are Black Ribbons Worn and Torn at a Jewish Funeral?

This ritual known as "Keriah" from the Hebrew word meaning "rent" or "torn" stems from the custom in Biblical times when mourners rent their garments, put on sackcloth and poured ashes upon their heads, as an outward sign of bereavement. There are numerous references to the custom in the Bible (Joshua 7.6 etc.). It has since been refined and modified so that today traditional Jews observe it by pinning a piece of black ribbon on the bereaved's garment and cutting it instead of the actual garment. The cut ribbon serves as an outward sign of mourning. Reform Jews have dispensed with this form of ritual.

What Is the Significance of Covering Mirrors in a House of Mourning?

Some say that traditionalist Jews do so during "shivah," the seven-day mourning period, "because the Rabbis taught that a mirror is a symbol of vanity and in times of mourning one should be made conscious of the vanity of earthly things and recognize only the abiding worth of spiritual values."

Some claim that it is a matter of superstition. The reflection of a coffin in a mirror was interpreted as betokening a second death. Mirrors were accordingly covered as a precautionary measure. Another notion is that mirrors attract evil spirits.

This custom has no hold on Liberal Jews.

Is It Permissible to Visit the Cemetery on the Sabbath?

No, no more than are burials permitted on the Sabbath.

77

VI. General

What Is "Kiddush Ha-shem"?

Kiddush (sanctification of), *Ha-shem* (the Name), is the term applied to Jewish martyrdom. It connotes surrendering one's life rather than desecrating the Name of God through renunciation, transgression of the Torah or the like.

What Does Being "a Good Jew" Mean?

There *is* a difference between *a good individual* and *a good Jew*. A good Jew is obliged to fulfill the requirements of Jewish religious discipline. This involves affiliation with a temple or synagogue and attendance at its Worship Services regularly. For the Sabbath, solemn assemblies and prayer are indispensable to Jewish religious life. One may be a good individual without attending Worship Services. But one cannot be a good Jew unless one does attend.

Being a good Jew also means to study, to acquire a knowledge of the Jewish past, to become aware of the realities of the Jewish present, and to assume responsibility for the advancement of Jewish life in the future. It means to rear one's children as Jews, giving them a Jewish education and instilling within them a proper sense of Jewish values. It means to make one's home Jewish. A *good Jew* is expected to be charitable and ethical and socially just.

What Can Jews Do About Anti-Semitism?

The disease of anti-Semitism is essentially a non-Jewish problem. However, there are some things which Jews can do, and are doing, to help make better non-Jews. In sponsoring the Jewish Chautauqua Society, for example, the National Federation of Temple Brotherhoods is doing much to create better understanding of Judaism through education: by sending rabbis to lecture at more than 1000 colleges and 350 Christian church camps, by donating thousands of Jewish reference books to college libraries, all on invitation, and by producing motion pictures for TV and group showings. Radio programs like "The Eternal Light," sponsored by the Jewish Theological Seminary, and "The Message of Israel," sponsored by the Union of American Hebrew Congregations, help to engender essential understanding.

"It is not our differences which divide us most bitterly," said the Rev. Donald Harrington, minister of The Community Church, New York City, "but differences which are not understood."

Jews can help non-Jews to understand and appreciate the beauties of Jewish ceremonies by inviting them occasionally to attend Worship Services in Temple and Synagogue. The Union of American Hebrew Congregations is doing a noble job in conducting many Institutes for the Christian Clergy, bringing outstanding rabbis into close contact with the ministers of the community in informative seminars.

Jews should resist all manifestations of anti-Semitism with determination and patience. They have every reason to be proud to be Jews. Jews should insist on full equality for themselves and for all other minorities, as well, not only for their own protection and self-respect, but to help strengthen democracy.

Moreover, since most prejudice is based on ignorance, Jews can do much to combat it as individuals through more study of their great Jewish heritage. Then will they be in a better position to provide proper information, about which their non-Jewish neighbors are often curious. Then will they be good ambassadors of their faith. They who can demonstrate that Judaism helps one to become a better person, will prove that it is a faith to be commended rather than condemned.

EPILOGUE

To Non-Jews

IF YOU HAVE FURTHER QUESTIONS ABOUT JUDAISM, OR A NEED FOR MORE INFORMATION ABOUT THE QUESTIONS ANSWERED IN THIS BOOK, WHAT WOULD YOU DO? WHAT COULD YOU DO?

The best thing to do at all times is to consult a reliable source. Don't rely on "hearsay" or the answers of any who evince uncertainty. Many good books are available to you. Reading will give you the facts. You may also find your nearest rabbi very helpful. Or you might write to the Department of Public Information, Union of American Hebrew Congregations, 838 Fifth Avenue, New York 21, New York.

To Jews

IF ANY OF THE QUESTIONS CONTAINED IN THIS BOOK, OR SIMILAR ONES WERE ASKED OF YOU AND YOU FELT AT A LOSS TO ANSWER CORRECTLY, WHAT WOULD YOU DO? WHAT COULD YOU DO?

The proper thing to do at all times is to be honest. If you know that you do not have the facts, admit it and offer to get them from a reliable source. By all means do not concoct an answer to spare yourself embarrassment. A mark of intelligence is to say "I don't know" when you don't know and to follow this up with the reading that will give you the answer. Or you might consult your rabbi.

98251